JOHNS HOPKINS UNIVERSITY STUDIES
IN
HISTORICAL AND POLITICAL SCIENCE

HERBERT B. ADAMS, Editor

History is past Politics and Politics present History—*Freeman*

TENTH SERIES

X-XI

COLUMBUS AND HIS DISCOVERY

OF

AMERICA

BY HERBERT B. ADAMS, PH. D., and HENRY WOOD, PH. D.
Professors in the Johns Hopkins University.

BALTIMORE
THE JOHNS HOPKINS PRESS
October and November, 1892

COPYRIGHT, 1892, BY THE JOHNS HOPKINS PRESS.

JOHN MURPHY & CO, PRINTERS,
BALTIMORE.

Printing Statement:

Due to the very old age and scarcity of this book, many of the pages may be hard to read due to the blurring of the original text, possible missing pages, missing text, dark backgrounds and other issues beyond our control.

Because this is such an important and rare work, we believe it is best to reproduce this book regardless of its original condition.

Thank you for your understanding.

CONTENTS.

		PAGE.
I.	Oration by Professor Herbert B. Adams......................................	7
II.	Oration by Professor Henry Wood..	40
III.	The First Jew in America, by Professor M. Kayserling,	45
IV.	Columbus in Oriental Literature, by Dr. Cyrus Adler,	51

APPENDIX.

I.	Bibliographies of the Discovery of America, by Charles Weathers Bump........	55
II.	Public Memorials of Columbus, by Charles Weathers Bump......................	69

COLUMBUS AND HIS DISCOVERY OF AMERICA.

I.[1]

"Was this his face, and these the finding eyes
    That plucked a new world from the rolling seas?
Who, serving Christ, whom most he sought to please,
    Willed his one thought until he saw arise
Man's other home and earthly paradise—
    His early vision, when with stalwart knees
He pushed the boat from his young olive-trees,
    And sailed to wrest the secret of the skies?

"He on the waters dared to set his feet,
    And through believing planted earth's last race.
What faith in man must in our new world beat,
    Thinking how once he saw before his face
The West and all the host of stars retreat
    Into the silent infinite of space!"[2]

Those faithful, finding eyes of Columbus! For now four hundred years they have looked outward upon the westward

---

[1] This address, by Professor Herbert B. Adams, was given at the Peabody Institute, Monday evening, October 10, 1892, to the officers and students of the Johns Hopkins University, and their friends, at the opening of the seventeenth academic year.

[2] This noble poem, "On a Portrait of Columbus," by Professor George E. Woodberry, of Columbia College, first appeared in *The Century Magazine*, May, 1892. The fine portrait which accompanied Mr. Woodberry's poem in that number was a copy of the "Columbus" now preserved in the Museum of the Ministry of Marine at Madrid. The picture was shown in enlarged form to the audience during the reading of the poem and the paragraph immediately following it.

course of empire in the new hemisphere which he first opened to discovery and conquest. Our modern eyes seek in vain to arrest that steadfast, far-away gaze, which seems to be looking into a future beyond our own. In the radiant light of the four hundredth anniversary of the discovery of America, millions of men and women will look upon this man's face with curious or admiring eyes; but when this generation, and many hundred years shall have passed away, those "finding eyes" will still be shining on through art, and poetry and history, like stars in the firmament.

There is a certain immortality in a great deed, like that of Columbus, which makes the doer, even though in many respects an ordinary man of his time, forever memorable. The discovery of America has been called the greatest event in secular history. This dictum may shock the ancients and startle the moderns; but let the mind of reflecting students range at will, through the centuries, back and forth in the galleries of human achievement, and determine if you can what single secular deed even approximates in grandeur and far-reaching historic significance to the finding of a new world on this earth, with which planet alone history is concerned. What are all the conquests of antiquity, or the decisive battles and great inventions of mankind, compared with America, time's noblest offspring? The passage of Christopher Columbus across the western sea, bearing the weight of Christendom and European civilization, opened the way for the greatest migrations in human history, for the steady march of enlightened nations towards civil and religious liberty. The discovery of America was the first crossing of Oceanus, that great and murmuring stream, which flowed around the old Mediterranean world. Amid the groaning and travailing of human creation, men burst the confines of that outward sea and began to people new continents. I tell you, sirs, the modern history of Europe, with its long exodus of hungry, landless peoples, with its epoch-making wars, its revolutions in church and state, were conditioned by that one secular event called the discovery of America.

Great deeds in history do not, however, stand alone. High mountains, grand and imposing though they may seem to the distant beholder, are after all simply conspicuous parts of our common earth. The loftiest peaks descend gradually to foot-hills, upland plateaus, lower plains, and finally to the level of the all-uniting sea. Nothing is isolated in nature or in human achievement. Great discoverers are like mountain-climbers, who by the aid of material vantage-ground and human experience, ascend height upon height until at last they stand like stout Balboa, when, silent upon a peak in Darien, with eagle eye he stared at the Pacific.

The discovery of America was foreordained from the beginning of the old classic world, when geographical science first began to move, "but slowly, slowly, creeping on from point to point," around the headlands of the Mediterranean Sea. Six hundred years B. C. the bold Phœnician sailors, under Egyptian auspices, circumnavigated Africa, sailing from East to West around what we now call the Cape of Good Hope, and returning in three years past the pillars of Hercules, through the straits of Gibraltar. Five hundred years before Christ, Hanno, the Carthaginian, anticipated the Portuguese discovery of the Canary Islands and the west coast of Africa.

Pythagoras and the Greek philosophers taught that the world is round. Plato, inspired by current traditions, based perhaps on physical facts, wrote in his dialogues of the continent of Atlantis, which had been submerged in the western sea. Aristotle believed that the inhabited earth, *oikoumenê gê*, was only one of several continents. He had the correct theory of the globe. Indeed, all modern discovery was anticipated in the following scientific statement: "In common speech," says Aristotle, "we speak of our world (*óikoumenê*) as divided into continents and islands. This is wrong. The *oikoumenê*, as known to us, is really a single island, lying in the midst of the Atlantic. Probably there are other similar *oikoumenai*, some larger than ours, some smaller, separated from it by the sea."

In his treatise on the Heavens (ii, 14), Aristotle said "those persons who connect the region in the neighborhood of the Pillars of Hercules with that towards India, and who assert that in this way the sea is *one*, do not assert things very improbable." Here is a full-orbed scientific idea which finally conquered and possessed the round world.[1] Greek thought was prophetic. Greek history foreshadowed the history of Europe, which is simply a greater Hellas, as America is an imperial and transatlantic Magna Graecia. Nothing of Greece doth fade but suffers a sea-change into something rich and strange. All our modern discoveries, colonization, politics, art, education, civilization, Christendom, the Oikoumenê, the great globe itself, are simply Greek ideas enlarged by historic processes of development.

> "The word unto the prophet spoken
> Was writ on tables yet unbroken;
> The word by seers or sibyls told,
> In groves of oak, or fanes of gold,
> Still floats upon the morning wind,
> Still whispers to the willing mind.

---

[1] "Greek speculation survived, though it missed reduction into practice. Strabo, who was master of all the geographical fact and theory of his time, was not likely to neglect Aristotle's memorable conjecture of more *oikoumenai* than one. With almost prophetic insight, he even improved on it. Besides a Terra Australis, such as Aristotle had indicated, he clearly foreshadowed the discovery of a Terra Occidentalis, occupying the same latitudes as the old *oikoumenê* itself. 'Possibly,' he says, 'the same temperate zone may contain two or more *oikoumenai*. It is even likely that such are to be found in the parallel of Athens.' Were this the case, the physical objection to the practicability of a westward voyage to India would probably cease: for the new *oikoumenai* might serve as stepping-stones to the westward explorer. This remarkable anticipation goes far to justify the words of an enthusiastic modern geographer, who declares that the nations of Europe from remote antiquity were gifted with a divine intuition which revealed to them another great world beyond their horizon, and whispered that this world was their natural patrimony. Aristotle had guessed at the plurality of *oikoumenai*: Strabo suggested the existence of another *oikoumenê* occupying the same latitudes as the old world, that is, the existence of America." (*History of the New World Called America*, vol. I, pp. 36–37, by Edward John Payne.) Strabo, i, 31, quoting Krates, speaks of the western voyage of Menelaos from Gades to India (Dr. A. Gudeman, Philological Association, J. H. U.)

We have been taught that Hebrew prophecy was history and Hebrew history was prophecy. There is a remarkable verse from Seneca, who has won eternal fame from Clio for these few words, once prophetic now historic:

> Venient annis saecula seris,
> Quibus Oceanus vincula rerum
> Laxet, et ingens pateat tellus,
> Tethysque novos detegat orbes,
> Nec sit terris ultima Thule.
> —*Medea*, 378–382.

In the Columbian library at Valladolid there is a copy of Seneca's tragedies published at Venice in 1510. Upon the margin of the verse from the Medea which has been quoted, Ferdinand, the son of Columbus, wrote in Latin, "This prophecy was fulfilled by my father, Christopher Columbus, the admiral, in 1492."

Dante was the poet-prophet of the Middle Ages and the historian of ancient culture. In the twenty-sixth canto of the Inferno, the Italian poet, under the guidance of the Latin Virgil, meets Odysseus, the Grecian type of Columbus, the adventurous navigator, who had sailed every sea. To Dante Odysseus narrates how once he and his companions steered westward past the pillars of Hercules, out upon the ocean, seeking a new world.

> "'O brothers, who amid a hundred thousand
> Perils,' I said, 'have come unto the West,
> Be ye unwilling to deny the knowledge,
> Following the sun, of the unpeopled world.
> Consider ye the seed from which ye sprang;
> Ye were not made to live like unto brutes,
> But for pursuit of virtue and knowledge.'
> So eager did I render my companions
> With this brief exhortation for the voyage,
> That then I hardly could have held them back."

They rowed away from the morning and made wings of their oars for a mad flight into another hemisphere. They came at last to a high mountain and a new land, but there arose a whirlwind and it smote upon the ship. Three times the vessel whirled about and then sank beneath the sea with all on board. Thus Odysseus and his companions came into the under world.

One century after the time of Dante there lived in the republic of Florence another poet-prophet, a contemporary of Savonarola and of Columbus. In a poem called the Greater Morning, Morgante Maggiore, this poet Pulci, who died five years before the discovery of America, made this remarkable prophecy, translated by Prescott in his "Ferdinand and Isabella," Vol. II, 117:

> "his bark
> The daring mariner shall urge far o'er
> The Western wave, a smooth and level plain,
> Albeit the earth is fashioned like a wheel.
> Man was in ancient days of grosser mould,
> And Hercules might blush to learn how far
> Beyond the limits he had vainly set
> The dullest sea-boat soon shall wing her way.
> Men shall descry another hemisphere,
> Since to one common centre all things tend;
> So earth, by curious mystery divine,
> Well balanced hangs amid the starry spheres.
> At our Antipodes are cities, states
> And thronged empires ne'er divined of yore."
> —Pulci, *Morgante Maggiore, Canto* 25: 22.

Turning from the poet-prophets, let us briefly notice the relation of schoolmen, churchmen, and scientific men to Columbus. In the year 1267 a Franciscan friar at Oxford collected from classical, Arabian and Hebrew literature the chief arguments concerning the possibility of reaching Asia by sailing westward from Europe. This Franciscan was Roger Bacon, the scholastic forerunner of Lord Bacon and a pioneer of experimental methods in science and philosophy. In his Opus Majus the great schoolman of Oxford wrote the following extraordinary summary of the best scientific views of the world's geography: "Aristotle says that there is not much ocean between the western parts of Spain and the eastern parts of India. He thinks that more than a fourth part of the surface of the globe is habitable. Averrhoes confirms this. Seneca says that this sea might be crossed in a few days with a favorable wind. Pliny says that people have actually sailed from the Arabian Gulf to Cadiz. Now the Arabian Gulf is a whole year's voyage from the Indian sea, so that it is clear that the eastern extremity of Asia cannot be a long way from us. The sea between Spain and Asia at any rate cannot possibly cover three-fourths of the surface of the globe. Besides, it is written in the fourth Book of Esdras, that six parts of the earth are habitable, and the seventh is covered with water. . . . Therefore I say that though the *oikoumené* of Ptolemy be confined within one-fourth of the globe's surface, more of that surface is really habitable. Aristotle must have known more than other people, because by Alexander's favor he sent out two thousand men to enquire about these matters. So must Seneca; for the Emperor Nero sent out people to explore in the same way. From all this it follows that the habitable surface of the earth must be considerable, and that which is covered with water but small."

In the year 1410, nearly one hundred and fifty years after Roger Bacon penned this remarkable passage, a famous churchman, Cardinal D'Ailly, Bishop of Cambrai, wrote an encyclopædic work called the *Imago Mundi*, in which all this geographical information is carefully repeated from the learned Franciscan of Oxford. Cardinal D'Ailly was president of the ecclesiastical commission which condemned John Huss to the stake in the year 1415, but that book called the *Imago Mundi* kindled in Spain a beaconlight which shot across the western sea. The book was not published until the year 1490 but manuscript copies of it were widely known in the second half of the fifteenth century. Doubtless Columbus, who could read Latin, was an early student of the Cardinal's work. Indeed Columbus owned a printed copy of this famous book and it is still preserved in the Columbian library at Seville with his own marginal notes.

The influence upon Columbus of his reading upon the subject of physical geography is clearly indicated in the following extract from the narrative of his third voyage, sent to Ferdinand and Isabella from the Island of Hispaniola: "I have always read, that the world comprising the land and the water was spherical, and the recorded experiences of Ptolemy and all others, have proved this by the eclipses of the moon, and other observations made from east to west, as well as by the elevation of the pole from north to south. But as I have already described, I have now seen so much irregularity, that I have come to another conclusion respecting the earth, namely, that it is not round as they describe, but of the form of a pear, which is very round except where the stalk grows, at which part it is most prominent."[1]

In one of his letters Columbus thus summarizes his reading of classical and Arabian authorities through the medium of the *Imago Mundi* of Cardinal D'Ailly: "Pliny writes that the sea and land together form a sphere, but that the ocean forms the greatest mass, and lies uppermost, while the earth is below and supports the ocean, and that the two afford a mutual support to each other, as the kernel of a nut is confined by its shell. The Master of scholastic history, in commenting upon Genesis, says, that the waters are not very extensive; and that although when they were first created they covered the earth, they were yet vaporous like a cloud, and that afterwards they became condensed, and occupied but small space: and in this notion Nicolas de Lira agrees. Aristotle says that the world is small, and the water very limited in extent, and that it is easy to pass from Spain to the Indies; and this is confirmed by Averrhoes, and by the Cardinal Pedro de Aliaco, who, in supporting this opinion,

---

[1] *Select Letters of Christopher Columbus*, translated and edited by R. H. Major, p. 134. Edition of 1870.

shows that it agrees with that of Seneca, and says that Aristotle had been enabled to gain information respecting the world by means of Alexander the Great, and Seneca by means of the Emperor Nero, and Pliny through the Romans; all of them having expended large sums of money, and employed a vast number of people, in diligent inquiry concerning the secrets of the world, and in spreading abroad the knowledge thus obtained. The said cardinal allows to these writers greater authority than to Ptolemy, and other Greeks and Arabs; and in confirmation of their opinion concerning the small quantity of water on the surface of the globe, and the limited amount of land covered by that water, in comparison of what had been related on the authority of Ptolemy and his disciples, he finds a passage in the third book of Esdras, where that sacred writer says, that of seven parts of the world six are discovered, and the other is covered with water."[1]

All science, like all literature, simply combines existing elements into fresh forms. Columbus breathed upon the dry bones of ancient and mediaeval geography, and they sprang together into vital form. A towering genius for discovery, beckoning him westward, seemed to arise before the mind's eye of that simple Genoese sailor, as he read the pages of the *Imago Mundi*, in which the geographical wisdom of the ancients had drifted to the western shore of Europe. Mr. Winsor, in his critical work on "Christopher Columbus: how he received and imparted the spirit of discovery," says, p. 457: "Bacon it was who gave that tendency to thought which, seized by Cardinal Pierre D'Ailly, and incorporated by him in his *Imago Mundi* (1410), became the link between Bacon and Columbus."

In an address before the Royal Geographical Society, in June, 1892, Mr. Clements R. Markham, an English naval officer, and a leading authority upon Columbus, represents him as one of the most skilful navigators of his time. The

---

[1] *Select Letters of Christopher Columbus*, pp. 144–146.

republic of Genoa was the centre of nautical science, and Columbus early became versed in all the mathematical and astronomical knowledge necessary for a good pilot and captain. It is very doubtful whether Columbus was educated, as some have said, at the University of Pavia; but he was an intelligent student and a persistent reader of cosmographical science. In 1501 he wrote: "At a very early age I became a sailor, and a sailor I have been ever since. . . . For forty years have I followed this calling. Whithersoever men have sailed to this day, thither have I also sailed. I have held traffic and converse with the wise and prudent, churchmen and laymen, Latins and Greeks, Jews and Moors. . . . During this time have I seen and made it my study to see, all writings, cosmography, histories, chronicles, philosophy and other arts, so that the hand of the Lord plainly opened my understanding to see that it was possible to sail from hence to the Indies, and set on fire my will for the execution thereof."

Columbus went to Portugal in 1472, at the age of 25. He went as young men now go to Chicago and the west. Lisbon was a city of enterprise and bold endeavor. For more than a hundred years skilful Genoese pilots, the best navigators of their time, had been in the service of the Portuguese government. They had found anew those long-lost sunset Islands of the Blest, now known as the Madeira and Canary Islands. Genoese sailors had even discovered the Azores, a thousand miles to the westward, half way across the broad Atlantic. Down the western coast of Africa had pushed those bold pilots from Genoa in the service of the most western State in continental Europe. Already in the thirteenth century Portuguese expeditions had passed Cape Non, a promontory so dangerous to navigators that men used grimly to say, "Whoever passes Cape Non will return or *not*." In 1435 Cape Bojador was doubled, and thus headland after headland was conquered as Portuguese discovery crept past Cape Blanco, Cape Verde and ever southwards to the region of Sierra Leone, where Hanno, the Carthaginian, had seen negroes and gorillas two thousand years before. What motives lured men ever onward? Love of adventure, the hunt for gold, the trade in slaves and ivory. The Phoenicians, the Carthaginians, the Arabians, and the Moors had all been engaged in the business of slave dealing. The Mohammedans taught it to the Portuguese and they taught it to the English.

A noble, scientific example to Columbus was his early contemporary, Prince Henry, the navigator, who sought a new route to India by way of the west coast of Africa. He had established a naval observatory at Sagres, the land's end of Portugal, the Sacred Promontory of the ancients, who supposed it to be the point farthest west on the habitable earth. There Prince Henry founded not only an observatory, but a school of geography. Thither like sea-gulls around a light-house flocked scholars, teachers, map-makers, and adventurous mariners. There, says John Fiske in his Discovery of America, I, 319, Prince Henry "spent the greater part of his life; thence he sent forth his captains to plough the southern seas; and as year after year the weather-beaten ships returned from their venturesome pilgrimage, the first glimpse of home that greeted them was likely to be the beacon-light in the tower where the master sat poring over problems of Archimedes or watching the stars."

Was there ever such a seminary for the training of geographers and discoverers of new lands? Prince Henry died in 1463, nine years before Columbus came to Portugal, but that scientific and adventurous spirit lived on in Lisbon, which was now the centre of geographical science. Bartholomew, the brother of Columbus, was already established there as a maker and publisher of maps recording Portuguese discoveries. Columbus himself was skilled in this art. He once said, "God gave me ingenuity and skill in designing charts and inscribing upon them, in the proper places, cities, rivers, mountains, isles, and ports." Indeed, he joined in many of those Portuguese maritime expeditions, and speaks of voyages to Guinea. Shortly before Columbus came to Lisbon, two Portuguese noblemen, Santaren and Escobar, had sailed down the Gold Coast and crossed the equator. Thence the land was found to bear away southwards. The Portuguese began to despair of ever doubling the continent of Africa and of reaching India by an eastern route.

Just here the grand idea of Columbus, of Cardinal D'Ailly, of Roger Bacon, and of Aristotle sprang into new life. It became clear to the Genoese pilot that the problem of a quick route to India was to be solved not by further and interminable groping down the African coast, but by boldly sailing westward around the globe. In 1474 the King of Portugal sought the advice of Paul Toscanelli, the great physicist in the republic of Florence, concerning a possible route to India. Shortly afterwards Columbus appealed to the same authority, and Toscanelli's answer is preserved. It is a clear and scientific statement of the whole case:

"Paul, the physicist, to Christopher Columbus, greeting. I perceive your great and noble desire to go to the place where the spices grow; wherefore in reply to a letter of yours, I send you a copy of another letter, which I wrote some time ago to a friend of mine, a gentleman of the household of the most gracious King of Portugal, . . . in reply to another, which by command of His Highness he wrote me concerning that matter: and I send you another sailing chart, similar to the one I sent him, by which your demands will be satisfied. The copy of that letter of mine is as follows:

"Paul, the physicist, to Fernando Martinez, canon, at Lisbon, greeting. . . . I have formerly spoken with you about a shorter route to the places of Spices by ocean navigation than that which you are pursuing by Guinea. The most gracious king now desires from me some statement, or rather an exhibition to the eye, so that even slightly educated persons can grasp and comprehend that route. Although I am well aware that this can be proved from the spherical shape of the earth, nevertheless, in order to make the point clearer and to facilitate the enterprise, I have decided to exhibit that route by means of a sailing chart. I therefore send to his majesty a chart made by my own hands, upon which are laid down your coasts, and the islands from which you must begin to shape your course steadily westward, and the places at which you are bound to arrive, and how far from the pole or from the equator you ought to keep away. . . . Do not wonder at my calling *west* the parts where the spices are, whereas they are commonly called *east*, because to persons sailing persistently westward those parts will be found by courses on the under side of the earth."[1]

Toscanelli's letter gives an elaborate and glowing description of the wealth of Cathay, the populous country of the Great Khan or King of Kings. "This country is worth seeking by the Latins, not only because great treasures may be obtained from it,—gold, silver, and all sorts of jewels and spices,—but on account of its learned men, philosophers and skilled astrologers." Toscanelli like Solomon was loyal to science and thus associated wisdom with rubies. He also expressed a commendable modern interest in the politics and administration of the country of Great Khan. In conclusion the Florentine professor of physics took special pains to inform Columbus that Lisbon was about 6,500 miles from "the great and splendid city of Quinsay," the Chinese King-see or Peking. From the island of Antilia to "the very splendid island of Cipango" it was only 2,500 miles. Toscanelli, following Marco Polo, said that island abounded "in gold, pearls, and precious stones, and they cover the temples and palaces with solid gold."

Marco Polo has been called "the true predecessor of Columbus." Polo spent seventeen years in China and was familiar with the geographical character of the Orient. He had been in the civil and diplomatic service of the Great Khan, whom he represented as the emperor of the far East. Upon his return to Europe Marco Polo gave a brilliant description of

---

[1] John Fiske, *Discovery of America*, Vol. I, p. 356.

the wealth of Cathay and especially of Zipango or Japan. Columbus became familiar with the writings of the Venetian traveller and it was the main object of the Genoese to reach the land of pearls and spices, the great archipelago comprising thousands of islands off the southeast coast of Asia.

Here we are at the bottom of the whole matter as it lay in the mind of Columbus. Away with idle talk about Vineland and the Norse Sagas, legends of northern discovery revived centuries after this era of Columbus. Although he did visit Iceland in 1477 he was now bent upon the discovery of the Zipango of Marco Polo and of more distant Cathay by a westward route according to the map and instructions of Toscanelli. That the Genoese pilot clearly apprehended the ideas of the Florentine physicist is perfectly apparent from another letter written by Toscanelli to Columbus. One extract tells us the whole story: "I regard as noble and grand your project of sailing from east to west according to the indications furnished by the map which I sent you, and which would appear still more plainly upon a sphere. I am much pleased to see that I have been well understood, and that the voyage has become not only possible but certain, fraught with honor as it must be and inestimable gain, and most lofty fame among all Christian people." The Italian physicist died in 1482, ten years before America was discovered.

Columbus first brought his project to the attention of King John of Portugal. It was by him referred to a joint commission of learned men and ecclesiastics, who declared that the scheme was altogether visionary and impracticable. The King's confessor, however, advised that the theory of Columbus be tested by a secret expedition. His charts were borrowed and the voyage was actually attempted, but it failed on account of the cowardice of the crew, who were beaten back by Atlantic storms. Columbus then went in disgust, and in some pecuniary embarrassment, to Spain in the year 1484 and there spent eight years in diligent propaganda of his noble scientific faith. It was condemned as heresy by narrow-minded men, who said there could not be any antipodes, or human beings on the other side of the world; for all men were descended from Adam and the known world had already been divided among his descendants. Moreover, if Columbus and his ships should sail down the watery slope towards the west, they could never get back again; it would be like sailing up a mountain. With such learned arguments did the wise men of Spain oppose the grand project of Columbus. But he made a few good friends among the more intelligent clergy. Most helpful of all during this long and discouraging period of neglect was Juan Perez, prior of the monastery at La Rabida, near Palos, where Columbus left his son Diego to be educated. "Let hatred and envy know," says Castelar, the Spanish statesman, "that the humble Franciscan monk, Juan Perez, in truth discovered the New World, through his deep friendship and admiration for Columbus." There was a women at court, the Marchioness de Moya, who befriended Columbus; and there was also a keen-witted Italian churchman, Geraldini, who said one day to Cardinal Mendoza, the Queen's confessor: "Good theologians are these critics of Columbus, but mighty poor cosmographers."

Into the wanderings of the Spanish court from city to city, into the long story of patient waiting and fruitless appeals for government-aid we need not enter here. The final triumph is closely associated with the surrender of the Alhambra and the Moorish capital by Boabdil to Ferdinand and Isabella. For more than seven hundred years the Christian powers of Spain had been struggling with the Moslem. Granada was the last stronghold of the infidel. For seven centuries Spain had held back the tide of Mohammedan invasion pouring in from the two continents of Africa and Asia. With this flood forever turned away from Western Europe, Spain was now ready to undertake the heroic enterprise of Columbus, to conquer and people a western world. Rather than to suffer rival France to profit by his scheme, the Spanish government appointed Columbus admiral, viceroy, governor-general of all islands and territories that he might discover beyond the seas. Money for the expedition came not from the sale of the Queen's jewels, as is commonly said, but from her husband's cash-box, on his wife's promise to repay. Ferdinand had been confiscating Jewish property in Aragon and expelling Israelites from the kingdom. Not jewels but Jews were the real financial basis of the first expedition of Columbus. The entire outfit cost about $100,000.

The Jews were expelled from Spain August 2, 1492. On the very next day Columbus sailed from Palos, with three vessels and men numbering in all about one hundred and twenty. Among them there was of course a clever Jewish interpreter who could speak Arabic, Coptic, Armenian, and other oriental languages. Columbus carried a Latin letter of introduction from Ferdinand and Isabella to the Great Khan. An historian went with the expedition to record the truth, a notary to draft treaties and attach all movable property in the West; a physician and a metallurgist were also on board. Curiously enough there sailed peaceably together on this first voyage to the New World an Irishman and an Englishman. The little fleet was detained at the Canary Islands until the sixth of September, when the admiral put out to sea from the harbor of Gomera and sailed west for nearly five weeks.

> "Behind him lay the gray Azores,
>   Behind the gates of Hercules;
> Before him not the ghost of shores;
>   Before him only shoreless seas.
> The good mate said: 'Now must we pray,
>   For lo! the very stars are gone.
> Speak, admiral! what shall I say?'
>   Why, say 'sail on! sail on! and on!'"

The great poets are after all the best historians. Antiquarians and critics sometimes grope blindly for the sunshine of truth in the wilderness of trees, through swamps and tangled undergrowth, while poets remain upon the hill-tops in the sunlit open under the full-orbed day, and look out over forest and fen to the sparkling sea. I have read many accounts of Columbus' first great voyage of discovery, but nowhere have I found so much of the real meaning of that world-historic event as in the Psalm of the West, by our own Baltimore and University poet, Sidney Lanier. The heroic spirit of Columbus speaks through these lines and the spirit giveth light:

"Ere we Gomera cleared, a coward cried,
 Turn, turn: here be three caravels ahead,
 From Portugal, to take us: we are dead!
Hold Westward, pilot, calmly I replied.
So when the last land down the horizon died,
 Go back, go back! they prayed: *our hearts are lead.—*
 Friends, we are bound into the West, I said.
Then passed the wreck of a mast upon our side.
 See (so they wept) *God's Warning! Admiral, turn!—*
 Steersman, I said, *hold straight into the West.*
Then down the night we saw the meteor burn.
 So do the very heavens in fire protest:
 Good Admiral, put about! O Spain, dear Spain!—
Hold straight into the West, I said again.

"Next drive we o'er the slimy-weeded sea.
 Lo! herebeneath (another coward cries)
 The cursèd land of sunk Atlantis lies:
This slime will suck us down—turn while thou'rt free!—
But no! I said, *Freedom bears West for me!*
 Yet when the long-time stagnant winds arise,
 And day by day the keel to westward flies,
My Good my people's Ill doth come to be:
 Ever the winds into the West do blow;
 Never a ship, once turned, might homeward go;
Meanwhile we speed into the lonesome main.
 For Christ's sake, parley, Admiral! Turn, before
 We sail outside all bounds of help from pain!—
Our help is in the West, I said once more.
 * * * * * *

"I marvel how mine eye, ranging the Night,
 From its big circling ever absently
 Returns, thou large low Star, to fix on thee.
Maria! Star? No star: a Light, a Light!
Wouldst leap ashore, Heart? Yonder burns—a Light

>   Pedro Gutierrez, wake! come up to me.
>   I prithee stand and gaze about the sea:
>   What seest? *Admiral, like as land—a Light!*
>   Well! Sanchez of Segovia, come and try:
>   What seest? *Admiral, naught but sea and sky!*
>   Well! But *I* saw it. Wait! the Pinta's gun!
>   Why, look, 'tis dawn, the land is clear: 'tis done!
>   Two dawns do break at once from Time's full hand—
>   God's, East—mine, West: good friends, behold my Land!"

An island was first seen in the moonlight at a distance of about six miles by a common sailor named Rodrigo de Triana, on board the Pinta, at about two o'clock in the morning. The journal of Columbus records that he himself and Pedro Gutierrez had seen the light moving up and down like a candle at about ten o'clock in the evening. Justin Winsor, in his recent work on Columbus (p. 510), maintains that he could not have seen a light, for if it had been ahead the discoverers would have stopped; if it had been abeam they would not have left it. According to the log-book of Columbus, he sailed straight on for four hours at the rate of twelve miles an hour. This was apparently reckless navigation for an experienced admiral who had seen a light off shore or on shore.

The apparent difficulty is solved by a theory of Rudolf Cronau, the latest German authority upon the landfall of Columbus. Cronau thinks that the three caravels sailed past the light and the island on the north or south side and in the morning found themselves on the west or lee side of Watling's Island, where they landed in a safe harbor now known as Riding Rocks. With a strong wind blowing from the east Columbus would not have dared to land anywhere except on the leeward side. The physical geography of Watling's Island has served to identify the landfall of Columbus and at the same time enables us to believe with Cronau that the watchful admiral may indeed have seen the moving light on the east side four hours before the sailor Roderigo discovered land on the west side. At any rate it was characteristic that the first enterprising American should have gone west for some distance before disembarking.

Columbus afterwards claimed and received the reward offered by the King and Queen for the discovery, because he had first seen the light. The poor sailor Roderigo de Triana thought himself wronged, and after his return to Spain he is said to have renounced Christianity and to have made his abode with the Mohammedans, " whom he regarded as a juster people." All of which goes to show what a faithful, honest soul Roderigo possessed and how high he valued his soul and his religion in comparison with a pension for the discovery of a new world.

In the Boston Public Library there is the Roman edition, the *editio princeps* of the first letter [1] of Columbus on his return to Spain, announcing the discovery of America. It is reproduced in fac-simile by the heliotype process in the Bulletin of the Library for October, 1890. It is the rarest work in American history, of which it is the true beginning. The following extract is from the translation by R. H. Major, editor of the *Select Letters of Columbus* (London, 1847, Publications of the Hakluyt Society). The letter is addressed to the lord of the treasury, Raphael Sanchez:

"Thirty-three days after my departure from Cadiz I reached the Indian Sea, where I discovered many islands, thickly peopled, of which I took possession without resistance in the name of our most illustrious Monarch, by public proclamation and with unfurled banners. To the first of these islands, which is called by the Indians Guanahani, I gave the name of the blessed Savior (San Salvador), relying upon whose protection I had reached this as well as the other islands; to each

---

[1] A fac-simile of the letter in Spanish of Christopher Columbus, written on his return from his first voyage and addressed to Luis de Sant Angel, 15 Feb.–14 March, 1493, announcing the discovery of the New World, was issued in 1889 by Ellis & Elvey, 29 New Bond Street, London, from a unique copy in the possession of Mr. Brayton Ives, of New York.

of these I also gave a name." Then follows a careful and most interesting description of the first expedition.

Columbus thought he had discovered certain islands lying off the eastern coast of Asia not far from Japan. He had no idea that he had approached an entirely new continent. " His discovery," says Mr. Winsor, " was a blunder; his blunder was a new world; the new world is his monument!" Harrisse, the best American authority upon Columbus, takes a liberal view of this historic blunder, which opened the way to the real truth regarding America. Harrisse likens the discovery by Columbus to the first detection of the planet Neptune by Le Verrier, the astronomer who announced that certain irregularities in the motion of Uranus were due to disturbing influences by some unknown body in the heavens. By following his suggestions, skilled observers found a new planet on the first of January 1847, and yet many of Le Verrier's original computations were found to be erroneous. So it was with the geographical calculations of Columbus. He had supposed that Japan was only about twenty-five hundred miles distant from the Canaries. Even Toscanelli, the great physicist of Italy, had blundered in extending Asia eastward upon his map by nearly the entire width of the Pacific Ocean, although he had calculated the earth's circumference within one hundred and twenty-four miles of the correct estimate.

If Columbus had known the true distance from the Canary Islands to Japan, probably he would never have dared to attempt a voyage of twelve thousand miles upon unknown seas. The historic blunder which he made was simply an historic necessity, like many other human mistakes in science and philosophy. The great contribution which Columbus made to human knowledge was that he demonstrated the existence of lands in the west, beyond the Atlantic Ocean and thus " linked forever the two worlds." Harrisse regards this discovery as the greatest in modern times. Alexander von Humboldt calls Columbus a giant standing on the confines between mediaeval and modern history and says "his existence marks one of the great epochs in the history of the world." Mr. Clements R. Markham maintains that all the discoveries made by other navigators, in the lifetime of Columbus, on the coasts of America, (except that of Cabral), were directly due to the first voyage of the admiral and should be classed as Columbian discoveries. Las Casas, a contemporary of Columbus, took the same historic view and said the admiral was the first to open the gates of ocean which had been closed for thousands of years. " It was he that put the thread into the hands of the rest by which they found the clue to more distant parts."

Modern critics of Columbus sometimes tell us that he began his maritime career as a pirate and a sea-rover. So did the Vikings of Scandinavia and the mariners of England. Spirits of the Danes and Norsemen! Shades of Drake and Hawkins! Who, if not pirates, were the original makers of Normandy and England? "Brave sea-captain," says Carlyle. "Norse sea-king—Columbus, my hero, royalest sea-king of all." Columbus, we are told, was a kidnapper and a slave-trader. So were all the great voyagers of his time. Even Prince Henry the Navigator supported his naval college at Sagres by the slave trade. Are we men of the nineteenth century so far removed from the treaty of Washington in 1842 which stopped the slave trade that we can talk reproachfully of it in the fifteenth century? Columbus, it is said, scornfully, was a seeker after gold.[1]

---

[1] We should not forget in the consideration of this gold-hunting spirit of Columbus, that he was driven on not only by the spirit of his time but by a natural desire to pay the expenses of his expedition and to satisfy the insatiable greed of his sovereign patrons. Personally he had a large ambition to use the spoil of the new world for the purpose of a new crusade. Savonarola and Columbus were in spirit among the last of the crusaders. The inroads of the Turks and the capture of Constantinople in 1453 inflamed mens' imaginations with schemes of oriental conquest and for the delivery of Jerusalem from the infidel. This crusading and religious spirit in Columbus was fostered by the long wars of Spain with the Mohammedans and by the final triumph of Ferdinand and Isabella over the Moorish kingdom of Granada in 1492.

What have men been doing since the beginning of the world or even since the Argonauts sailed westward to California in 1849? The poor Genoese pilot was ambitious. Ah, yes! Men do say that Caesar was ambitious. Columbus wanted, not a crown, but a vice-royalty in his island realm. What a craven he would have been, with his royal soul, to have accepted less power and honor than was accorded to Spanish admirals of his time.[1]

"I ought to be judged," said Columbus in one of his later letters, "as a captain sent from Spain to the Indies, to conquer a nation numerous and warlike, with customs and religion altogether different to ours; a people who dwell in the mountains, without regular habitations for themselves or for us; and where, by the Divine will, I have subdued another world to the dominion of the King and Queen, our sovereigns; in consequence of which, Spain, that used to be called poor, is

---

[1] In the prerogatives granted to Christopher Columbus by the King and Queen of Spain, at Granada, April 30, 1492, he was given the powers of viceroy and governor over the new lands that he might discover: "For as much as you, Christopher Columbus, are going by our command, with some of our vessels and men, to discover and subdue some Islands and Continent in the ocean, and it is hoped that by God's assistance, some of the said Islands and Continent in the ocean will be discovered and conquered by your means and conduct, therefore it is but just and reasonable, that since you expose yourself to such danger to serve us, you should be rewarded for it. And we being willing to honour and favour you for the reasons aforesaid; Our will is, That you, Christopher Columbus, after discovering and conquering the said Islands and Continent in the said ocean, or any of them, shall be our Admiral of the said Islands and Continent you shall so discover and conquer; and that you be our Admiral, Vice-Roy, and Governour in them, and that for the future, you may call and style yourself, D. Christopher Columbus, and that your sons and successors in the said employment, may call themselves Dons, Admirals, Vice-Roys, and Governours of them; and that you may exercise the office of Admiral, with the charge of Vice-Roy and Governour of the said Islands and Continent, which you and your Lieutenants shall conquer, and freely decide all causes, civil and criminal, appertaining to the said employment of Admiral, Vice-Roy, and Governour, as you shall think fit in justice, and as the Admirals of our kingdoms use to do."—*Charters and Constitutions of the U. S.*, Part I., p. 304.

now the most wealthy of kingdoms. I ought to be judged as a captain, who for so many years has borne arms, never quitting them for an instant. I ought to be judged by cavaliers who have themselves won the meed of victory; by knights of the sword and not of title deeds; as least, so it would have been among the Greeks and Romans, or any modern nation in which exists so much nobility as in Spain." [1]

Something of the haughty spirit of Cortes and Pizarro was in this Columbus of ours. By all accounts he was noble and even kingly in his appearance. He could not be false to his royal nature. Columbus is blamed for cruelty to his men. A commanding officer must sometimes be cruel in dealing with cut-throats, pirates, and mutineers. Columbus, we are told, did not succeed in ruling his colony and in preserving order. Possibly he was not cruel enough. Indeed Columbus was far too good a man for the company he kept and for the King he served. Columbus was loyal to his own standards of duty to church and State; but Ferdinand, the king who had proved false to both Moors and Jews, thought nothing of breaking his promise to Columbus. At the end of his third voyage he was superseded in office and was sent home to Spain a royal captive.

Tarducci[2] says of Columbus, "the chains in which he had been brought home as a prisoner from the New World, and which he had always kept hung up in his room as a memorial of the reward bestowed for his services, he directed to be placed in his sepulcher after his death; and his will was in this respect punctually executed. No one seemed aware of his passing away. The death of the discoverer of the New World [in 1506 at the age of fifty-nine][3] passed without notice within the walls of the city [Valladolid] where he died. . . .

---

[1] *Select Letters of Columbus*, pp. 169-170.

[2] Tarducci's *Life of Columbus*, p. 365.

[3] Mr. Clements R. Markham has determined by various lines of historical argument, that 1447 was the year of the birth of Columbus.

But the oblivion with which the malice of his enemies succeeded in surrounding his person was soon dispelled by the brilliant splendor of his fame, to which time gave ever-increasing strength and vigor. . . . King Ferdinand was forced to yield to the growing influence, and ordered a monument erected to the man he had caused to expire in poverty and anguish in a lodging house."[1]

The world has gone on building monuments and erecting statues in honor of Christopher Columbus. The popular heart beats truer than the pulse of princes or detractors. The fame of Columbus has been slowly maturing through the centuries, but it has blossomed gloriously after four hundred years. In 1792 Baltimore was the only American city possessing a monument in honor of the discoverer of the New World. This monument now stands on the grounds of the Samuel Ready Asylum, between North Avenue and the Harford Road. It is an obelisk, forty-four feet and four inches high. The base is six and a half feet square; the top is about two and a half feet square. The monument is made of brick and mortar, stuccoed or cemented on the outside so that it has the appearance of grey sandstone. Some of our resident Baltimoreans are not quite sure whether this modest shaft was not erected by Zenos Barnum in memory of a favorite horse;[2] but

---

[1] The low state to which Columbus was reduced at the time of his fourth voyage to America is described in the following extract from his letter to the King and Queen of Spain: "Such is my fate, that the twenty years of service through which I have passed with so much toil and danger, have profited me nothing, and at this very day I do not possess a roof in Spain that I can call my own; if I wish to eat or sleep, I have nowhere to go but to the inn or tavern, and most times lack wherewith to pay the bill. Another anxiety wrung my very heartstrings, which was the thought of my son Diego, whom I had left an orphan in Spain, and stripped of the honour and property which were due to him on my account, although I had looked upon it as a certainty, that your Majesties, as just and grateful Princes, would restore it to him in all respects with increase." (*Select Letters of Christopher Columbus*, p. 179).

[2] The origin of this extraordinary tradition, in which many honest people continue to believe, is possibly due to a popular confusion of the Columbus

others who are better informed indignantly reject such a shallow and vulgar tradition. The balance of probability is overwhelmingly against the notion of a horse named "Christopher Columbus" dying on the 12th of October, 1792, on the three hundredth anniversary of the discovery of America. The inscription on the west side of this monument is engraved upon a marble slab and reads as follows:

SACRED
TO THE
MEMORY
OF
CHRIS
COLUMBUS
Octob. XII
MDCCVIIIC.

The Roman numerals VIII are placed before the final C to indicate that they are to be subtracted from one hundred, thus leaving the date 1792. This archaic inscription is of itself sufficient evidence of the honest and historic purpose of the man who erected the monument. The managers of the Samuel Ready Asylum have a record of the ownership of their estate which has been traced back through Baltimore land records as far as 1787. In 1789 the property came into the possession of a Frenchman named Charles Francis Adrian le Paulmier Chevalier d'Anmour. To some critics and scoffers the unconscionable length of this name and a popular corruption of it into the form of *D'Amour* have made it seem fictitious, but the Chevalier D'Anmour was an historic character, who ought never to have been forgotten in our local history. He was the first French consul in Baltimore. He

---

monument with the Wilkens monument to a horse, in the western neighborhood of Baltimore on the Frederick road. This latter monument is, however, very modern.

is mentioned in the Journals of Congress as far back as October 27, 1778, soon after our first treaty with France. He was the first appointed consul in the State of Maryland, with a commission from Gérard, minister plenipotentiary and consul-general. In 1779 and 1780 D'Anmour's commission was extended to Virginia and North Carolina. In 1783 the Chevalier became consul-general of France for the State of Maryland, the Commonwealth of Virginia, and the States of North Carolina, South Carolina, and Georgia (See Journals of Congress, vol. III., 102, 330, 427; vol. IV., 263). In the Maryland Journal and Baltimore Advertiser of December 17, 1782, the following marriage is recorded: "The Honourable Le Chevalier D'Anmour, His Most Christian Majesty's Consul for the Middle District of the United States, to Miss Julia De Rocour, a young Lady lately arrived here from the West Indies." In the Journals of Congress the name is spelled in various ways,—D'Anemours, D'Annemours, and D'Anmour. The latter appears to be the phonetic form into which the original name was finally reduced.

It is clear from the land records of Baltimore that the Chevalier D'Anmour owned the estate upon which the Columbus monument, bearing the date 1792, now stands. The French consul acquired the property in 1789 and held it until 1796, when it passed into the hands of Archibald Campbell. In the library of the Maryland Historical Society there may be seen by any visitor a framed map of Baltimore, printed in 1801, showing the Campbell estate and upon it a picture of the monument in question. This simple fact ought to discredit forever the absurd popular tradition of a monument "*Sacred to the Memory*" of Zenos Barnum's horse. The Campbell estate did not come into the possession of the Barnum family until the year 1833—more than forty years after the Columbus monument was erected. The inscription October 12, 1792, upon a monument erected upon D'Anmour's own land and near his own house, ought to be taken at its face value as demonstrating the historic commemoration, by the generous and public spirited Chevalier, of the tercentenary of the discovery of America. The very existence of the monument with its marble tablet and historic inscription, proves that its founder was an admirer of Columbus and a friend of the land potentially discovered on that historic day, October 12, three centuries before. The important point which now remains for Baltimoreans to establish is this: their Columbus monument is probably the oldest[1] in the New World in honor of its discoverer.

Next to Baltimore comes Washington in point of priority in doing honor to Columbus in North America. The east

---

[1] In the appendix to this address Mr. Charles W. Bump, a graduate student of the Johns Hopkins University, has prepared a list of the various monuments to Columbus, with the aid of Mr. Frederick A. Ober, recently of the Latin American Department of the World's Columbian Exposition and special commissioner of the West Indies. From this list it will appear that the Baltimore monument to Columbus antedates the Havana monument by three years.

The existence of this Baltimore monument in memory of Columbus was first made known to Johns Hopkinsians in 1876, the opening year of the University, by its first librarian, Arthur Wellington Tyler, who in company with the present librarian, Mr. N. Murray, and his brother, Professor T. C. Murray, chanced one day while walking in the country to find this curious obelisk of brick and stucco in a grove of cedar trees, near the remains of some rude earth-works that had been hastily thrown up for the defence of Baltimore in the time of the late civil war. In 1876, North Avenue had not yet been opened and the monument stood at some distance from the nearest thoroughfare. The writer well remembers the mild excitement produced in a small academic circle by the startling announcement made by Mr. Tyler of his discovery of a monument to Christopher Columbus in the neighborhood of Baltimore. The historical department went out in a body of one, with the original discoverers, to see the obelisk and its remarkable inscription. It was the first archaeological discovery by Johns Hopkinsians and it created an historical enthusiasm akin to that of the Pickwick Club, when its founder discovered a Roman inscription, which, however, some skeptics interpreted as " Bil Stumps His Mark." Our ardor for Columbian inscriptions was somewhat dampened when we were told by native Baltimoreans that the " Chris Columbus " monument was erected in memory of a horse bearing that historic name. But to this day some of us have continued in our original faith and have steadfastly maintained that a

portico of the Capitol has broad stone steps flanked by large buttresses. On the south buttress there is a large marble group representing the discovery of America. It was executed by an Italian sculptor named Persico in 1846 at a cost of $40,000. Columbus is represented holding aloft a small globe inscribed "America," while at his side crouches an Indian maiden. The figure of Columbus is encased in armor. The bronze door, called the "Columbus Door" at the main entrance to the Capitol, was modelled at Rome in 1858 by Randolph Rogers, the American sculptor, and was cast in Munich in 1860. It is nineteen feet in height and nine feet wide. It weighs 20,000 pounds and cost $28,000. On it are designs

---

monument, bearing the inscription "Sacred to the Memory of Christopher Columbus, October 12, 1792" must be the memorial of a man and not of a beast, of an historic event and not of an equine death and burial.

The subject was first carefully investigated by a writer for the Baltimore *American*, November 19, 1880. The opening of Boundary Avenue had brought the old-time monument within plain view of passers-by. The contributor to *The American*, although born and reared within half a mile of the spot, said that he had never known, until three months before, of the existence of the monument. He proceeded to describe its location and appearance: "On the east side of the Harford turnpike, leading out of Baltimore City, adjoining what has for several years past been known as 'Darley Park,' about one and a half miles from the City Hall, has stood for a century past an old-fashioned, substantial and spacious mansion house, with numerous outbuildings, all of stone and old English brick. It is just discernible through the branches of numerous aged trees, at a distance of perhaps three hundred yards from the road. For half a century it has been known as the Barnum property, having been, and still being, in the possession of the family of that name, who were the founders of the famous Barnum's Hotel. Thirty or forty years ago the elder David Barnum resided here. The tract comprises about twenty-five acres, and the grounds around the old mansion house, although sadly out of repair since the death of David Barnum some twenty years ago, are still inviting and picturesque, with their box-wood walks, bordered roadways lined with rows of cedars, fine old fruit trees, and rosebush clusters here and there. In the rear, southeast corner of the enclosure stands the Columbus Monument, on an elevated plateau, which seems to have been artificially arranged."

The reporter then gave the legendary accounts of the monument, with various popular stories all manifestly inventions and absolutely untrust-

in high relief illustrative of the career of Columbus. The casing is covered with emblematic designs and on the top of the arch is a bust of Columbus. There are eight panels on the door and also a transom panel. On them the following scenes represent to the eye the life of our hero: the examination of Columbus before the Council of Salamanca; departure of Columbus from the convent of La Rabida for the Spanish Court; Columbus before the court of Ferdinand and Isabella; departure of Columbus from Palos on his first voyage of discovery; Columbus landing at San Salvador; first encounter of Columbus with the Indians; triumphal entrance of Co-

---

worthy; but, at the same time, he gave the correct and historic view, that the shaft was erected by the first French consul in Maryland, who had bought the estate upon which the monument now stands. "Early in the present century," the writer continues, "the property was owned by Thomas Tenant, a wealthy, influential and a leading citizen of Baltimore. One of his daughters, became the wife of Hon. John P. Kennedy. Another daughter is now living at an advanced age, in New York City, and only two years since paid a visit to the old homestead and sat beneath the shadow of the Columbus monument. She stated that it stood in her early childhood just as it stands now, and was often visited by noted Italians and Frenchmen, who seemed to know of it in Europe."

The subject of the Columbus monument was investigated anew by an undergraduate student of the Johns Hopkins University, Mr. Victor Rosewater, son of the editor of *The Omaha Bee*, which first published the young writer's results. They were afterward revised by him in New York and were republished in *Frank Leslie's Illustrated Weekly*, December 20, 1890. Rosewater's original article was accepted by Mr. William E. Curtis, of the Bureau of American Republics, and became the basis of an official account of the Baltimore monument and also of his recent article on "Columbus monuments," in *The Chautauquan* for November, 1892. Another article on the Baltimore monument to Columbus appeared in the *Baltimore American*, August 4, 1891.

The present writer is greatly indebted to Mr. Henry F. Thompson, of the Maryland Historical Society, for valuable information and references confirming the above historic view of the Columbus monument. Mr. Thompson lived in its immediate vicinity in his early life and is perfectly confident, from his own family traditions, that the shaft was erected in memory of the discoverer of America.

lumbus into Barcelona; Columbus in chains; death bed of Columbus.

In the National Museum at Washington there is a most interesting relic of Columbus, namely a piece of the bolt to which he was chained in the fortress at San Domingo. There is also to be seen in the National Museum an old door from the convent at La Rabida at Palos, where Columbus found shelter for himself and son with the good prior Juan Perez. At the World's Fair in Chicago there will be exhibited a magnificent collection of relics, photographs, and pictures illustrating Columbus and his time.

Many cities now have a Columbus statue. The Italian citizens of Baltimore have placed in our Druid Hill Park, a statue of their great countryman, by Achille Canessa. Philadelphia has a Columbus statue in her Fairmount Park. In New York, at the west entrance to Central Park, stands the noblest statue of the noble Genoese pilot. It was presented to the people of this country by the Italians of the United States, Canada, Mexico, and Central America. It is of Carrara marble, and was modelled by Gaetano Russo, an Italian sculptor in Rome. It is one of the finest works of modern Italian art. This international monument, with its granite base and column, stands seventy-five feet high. At the base of the column there is a statue of the genius of Italy bending over a globe and discovering a new continent. On the opposite side there is a representation of the American eagle holding the shields of Genoa and Spain. There are also two bronze reliefs upon the base, one picturing Columbus and his men when they first saw land and the other showing the first landing. At Madrid there is a fine statue of Columbus representing him in the solemn religious act of taking possession of the New World in the name of Christian Spain. He stands looking steadfastly upward, with the flag of Spain in his hand. In the city of Genoa there is the grandest monument in the world in honor of Columbus.

The various statues and portraits[1] of the great navigator have no uniform type; but what matters it whether we have the man's exact likeness in marble or on canvas? It is the ideal Columbus that the world wishes to commemorate. Purified and ennobled, his great soul has become again incarnate in the imagination of artists and of great peoples who unite to do him honor in this Columbian year.

Let no one regret that the New World was not named in honor of Columbus. As Pericles said of the Athenian generals slain : " The whole earth is the monument of illustrious men." The name "America" is a beautiful and worthy Germanic name meaning rich in industry, in active busy life. It was not an honor stolen from Columbus by Amerigo Vespucci, the Florentine, but it was bestowed by a German monk, Martin Waldseemüller, upon the land which Amerigo had so well described in his letters to the Medici. The motive was at once scientific and monkish. Europe, said Martin the geographer of the monastic college of San Dié, was named after a woman; let us have one continent named after a man.

The eternal womanly has risen triumphant and serene in " Columbia," the spirit of American liberty. It was no calamity for Columbus that he was prevented from becoming the viceroy, the Pizarro of the new world or from stamping his name upon a continent. In losing all, he gained all; and the Holy Mother Church will perhaps some day pronounce

---

[1] Pictures of some of the monuments and statues above mentioned and of certain portraits of Columbus were exhibited during the delivery of Dr. Adams' address. Among others was shown the Lotto portrait of Columbus, described by Mr. John C. Van Dyke in *The Century Magazine* for October, 1892.

In a recent address, October 26, before the Union League Club of Philadelphia, Mr. Chauncey M. Depew says that he met Columbus at the Chicago celebration and asked him if he was going to stay with us. "Well," he said, "after seeing about five hundred of my alleged portraits around this city, I have made up my mind to return."

him blessed. Happy already is this modern St. Christopher,[1] who brought the colonies of Christian Europe across the western sea.

One hundred years ago the discoverer of America was first publicly honored in this City of Baltimore. To-day we recall and apply to him the spirit of our own Baltimore motto, which by some curious historic chance has come down to us in the language of Italy and of Columbus. *Fatti maschii, parole femine*, manly deeds and womanly words, belong to the world-pilot of Genoa as well as to Lord Baltimore, the first great American apostle of tolerant opinion. The manliest deed in American history was that first great voyage of Columbus across an unknown, western sea. The generous and true-hearted words of our Baltimore poet have nobly characterized that great Italian who led the way to this larger world. The Psalm of the West by Sidney Lanier, the laureate of our University, who though dead will speak forevermore in words of music, is the noblest tribute to the historic memory of Christopher Columbus. We Hopkinsians honor the great Captain for his immortal deed, which first brought the old

---

[1] In connection with his book on *America; Its Geographical History*. (Extra Volume XIII of the Johns Hopkins University Studies.) Dr. Walter B. Scaife has brought out a fac-simile of the American portion of Juan de la Cosa's map of the world, 1500, representing also St. Christopher carrying the Christ-child across the sea. Mr. R. H. Major has used a chromolithograph of this picture as the frontispiece to his second edition (1870) of the *Select Letters of Columbus*. Mr. Major and others have suggested that St. Christopher represents Christopher Columbus carrying the Christian faith across the Atlantic, and that the face is a portrait. In corroboration of this idea, Mr. Major quotes Herrera's description: "Columbus was tall of stature, with a long and imposing visage. His nose was aquiline; his eyes blue; his complexion clear, and having a tendency to a glowing red; the beard and hair red in his youth, but his fatigues early turned them white." The late Henry Stevens once said that the Cosa map is the most precious cartographical document relating to the New World. This map was bought some years ago by the Queen of Spain and it is now in the Naval Museum at Madrid.

World into historical contact with the New. The light he saw—

> "It grew a starlit flag unfurled!
> It grew to be Time's burst of dawn.
> He gained a world; he gave that world
> Its grandest lesson: 'On and on!'"

What indomitable purpose was that of Columbus! It was steadily pursued through twenty years of ridicule, with at first only two men and two women who did not laugh at him,— Juan Perez the Franciscan, Diego Deza the Dominican, the Marchioness de Moya and Queen Isabella. Think of it! The organized forces of society, church, state, and university, all arrayed against him! But he mastered them all,—prelates, courtiers, and learned doctors of Spain. He conquered the prejudices of a thousand years and then died a martyr to his heroic cause. Christopher Columbus, the son of Italy, the heir of all the ages, he did this great and manly deed; he discovered a world. *He did it;* for that reason we honor him. He sacrificed all; and for this reason we love him.

"Men, my brothers, men the workers ever reaping something new;
That which they have done but earnest of the things which they shall do."

In the fields of science and religion, in art and letters, in civic and social reform, in the improvement of great peoples and in the elevation of mankind, there are still new worlds for discovery and conquest. The heavens above and the earth beneath and even the depths of the great sea are full of fresh materials for observation and research. The beauty of this rolling cosmos is that the infinitely small is as wonderful as the infinitely great. From the red planet Mars and the new moon of Jupiter to a microscopic germ of life or black death, the range of all scientific inquiry is equally noble and rewarding. Let us then, comrades all, press forward. As Aeneas said to his companions, "It is not too late to seek another world."

Printed by Libri Plureos GmbH in Hamburg, Germany